Dinosaurs

Experts on child reading levels
have consulted on the level of text and
concepts in this book.

At the end of the book is a "Look Back and Find" section
which provides additional information and encourages
the child to refer back to previous pages
for the answers to the questions posed.

First Paperback Edition 1990

Published in the United States in 1985 by
Franklin Watts, 95 Madison Avenue, New York, NY 10016

© Aladdin Books Ltd/Franklin Watts

Designed and produced by:
Aladdin Books Ltd, 28 Percy Street, London W1P 9FF

ISBN 0-531-15158-1

Printed in Belgium

FRANKLIN · WATTS · FIRST · LIBRARY

Dinosaurs

by
Kate Petty

Consultant
Angela Grunsell

Illustrated by
Alan Baker

Franklin Watts
London · New York · Toronto · Sydney

Have you ever tried to imagine what dinosaurs were really like? Millions of years ago hundreds of different dinosaurs ruled the world.

The bones of *Megalosaurus* were found in rocks millions of years after it died. From its skeleton we can work out what it was like when it was alive.

The name dinosaur means terrible lizard.
Have you ever seen a lizard or a crocodile?
They belong to a group of animals called reptiles.

Dinosaurs were reptiles too. Did you know that baby dinosaurs hatched from eggs?
All reptile babies come from eggs.

9

Dinosaurs lived in the world for 140 million years. Many of them were giants like this *Apatosaurus* but *Compsognathus* was no bigger than a hen.

These dinosaurs liked swampy places.
The dinosaur bird was called *Archaeopteryx*.
This spiky dinosaur was *Stegosaurus*.

Some very large dinosaurs ate only plants. *Diplodocus* had a long tail and a long neck. It nibbled at trees like a giraffe does.

Brachiosaurus was the biggest dinosaur.
It could have peered over
the top of your school.
It weighed as much as 50 elephants.

Stegosaurus looked fierce but it was a plant eater. The bony plates on its back and tail were to keep dinosaurs like this *Allosaurus* away.

14

Even the hungriest meat eaters must have thought twice before attacking spiky *Kentrosaurus.*

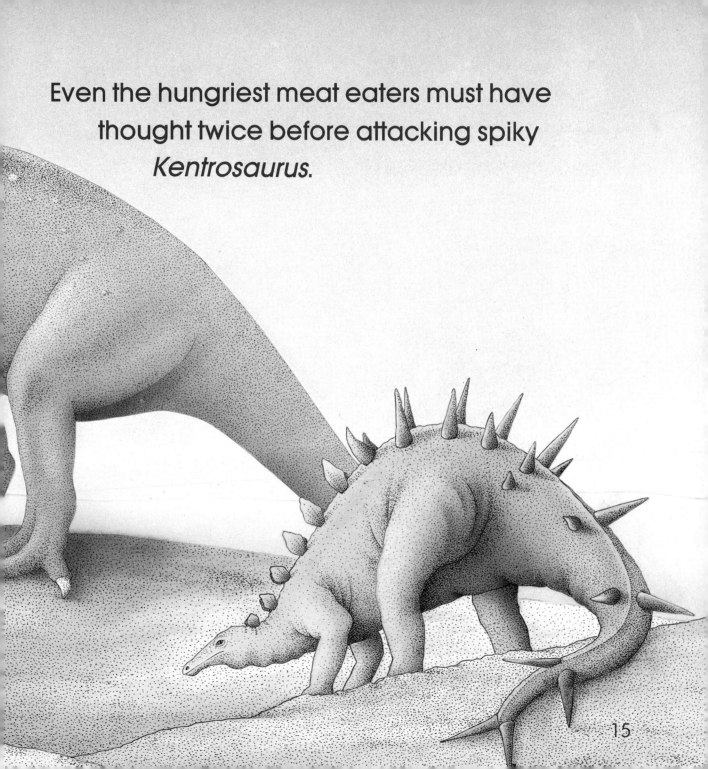

Tyrannosaurus was the largest meat-eating animal ever to live on earth.
Its head alone was as big as you are.
It gripped its prey with its huge back claws.

Deinonychus was smaller but just as vicious.
It used its curved claws to slash at its victims.

All these plant eaters were well protected. *Triceratops* had three sharp horns. A group of them together could hold off attackers.

Palaeoscenus could twist its body
and impale the enemy on its spikes.
An Ankylosaur could lash out with its strong tail.

Duck-billed dinosaurs took to the water to escape
their hunters. They had webbed feet.
Their jaws had 2,000 teeth to grind up
the twigs and pine needles they ate.

Bone-headed dinosaurs had skulls like crash helmets. They moved around in herds and butted each other like rams do. The strongest fighter was the leader of the herd.

Plesiosaurs and Ichthyosaurs were not dinosaurs. They were reptiles that lived in the sea when dinosaurs lived on land. *Plesiosaurus* had a long neck and sharp, pointed teeth for catching fish.

Ichthyosaurus was as big as a whale.

The flying *Pteranodon* wasn't a dinosaur either.

It was a reptile and had a furry body like a bat.

Archaeopteryx was the first real bird
even though it had teeth and a bony tail.
There are still birds today, but no dinosaurs.
Quite suddenly, about 65 million years ago,
all the dinosaurs disappeared from the Earth.
The reason for this is still a mystery.

In 1983 a man found this claw in a muddy claypit.
It is about as long as your arm. It came from a
dinosaur that no one had known about before.

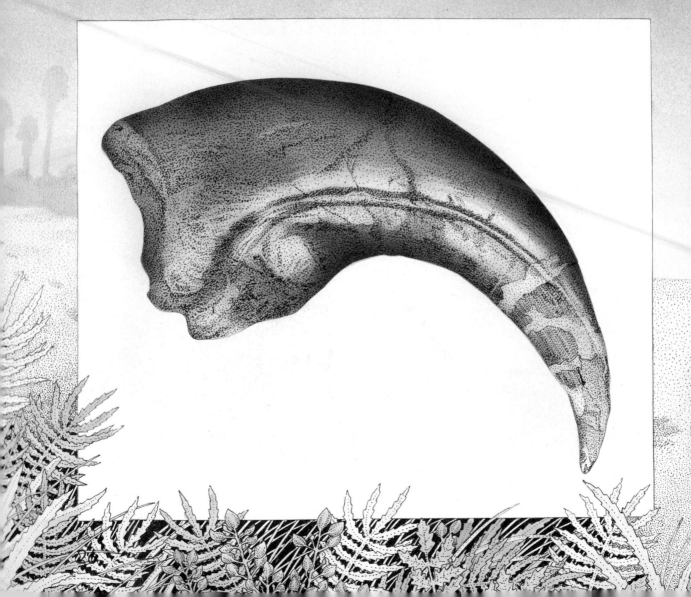

The footprints which this *Megalosaurus* left behind lasted for 100 million years. They were discovered in a stone quarry. Every new discovery helps us to imagine what dinosaurs were like.

Look back and find

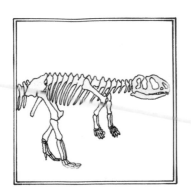

Why can't you go to see dinosaurs in a zoo?
Because all the dinosaurs died long before there were people on Earth.

What is the name for animal remains found buried in the rocks?
Fossils. Look out for fossils of shellfish in stones and rocks on the beach.

Human beings have been on the Earth for 3 million years. How long did dinosaurs live in the world?

Some dinosaurs lived in forests, others in deserts or near the sea. What sort of places did this dinosaur like?

What did *Allosaurus* eat?

Can you find a plant eating dinosaur?

Which of these animals eat meat: horse, rabbit, dog, cat, human?

How big was *Tyrannosaurus*?

How do we know what colors
dinosaurs were?
*We don't. We have to guess. Some
reptiles are brightly colored and
some match their surroundings.*

Why do you think duck-billed dinosaurs
had webbed feet?

What sort of animals have webbed feet now?

What do they use them for?

How are the birds we see now
different from *Archaeopteryx*?

Why do you think dinosaurs died out?
*Here are two suggestions. Perhaps the weather
became too hot for them. Perhaps their eggs
were eaten by other small animals.*

Index